A Celebration of Canada's Olympic Triumph

GOLDEN
Glory

WRITTEN BY THE SPORTS STAFF OF THE TORONTO STAR

TRIUMPH

Glory in Salt Lake

PHOTO GALLERY

*Photographs by
The Associated Press and
AllSport Photos USA*

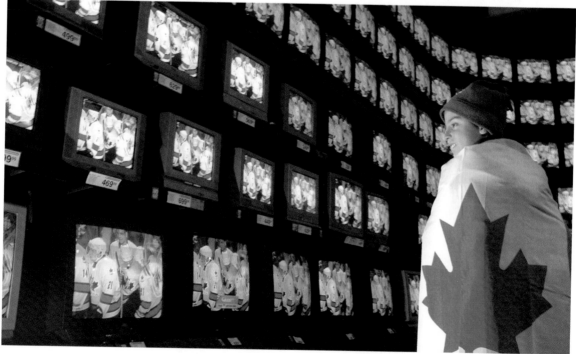

Permissions

Photo Credits:

Allsport USA
1, 13, 18-19, 22, 23, 24, 27, 29, 30-31, 32, 42-43, 52-53, 62, 63, 69-top, 69-bottom,
70-71, 73-top, 73-bottom, 74-all, 75-all, 76-77, 78-79.

The Associated Press
Front cover, 2-left, 2-3, 4, 5, 6-7, 8-top, 8-bottom, 9-top, 9-bottom, 11, 15, 17, 21, 28, 35, 36-37, 39, 40, 41,
44-45, 47, 48-49, 50, 51, 55, 56-57, 58-59, 61, 65, 66-67.

Cover and book design: Chris Kozlowski, Dallas, Tex.
Published by: Epic Sports, Birmingham, Ala.

Contents

Congrats for Gretzky

"It was an awesome game and we're so proud of you. All of Canada is cheering at this moment."

— **Prime Minister Jean Chretien, in conversation with Wayne Gretzky following Canada's gold medal win.**

CANADIAN PRESS

Following Team Canada's 5-2 win over the U.S., Wayne Gretzky, executive director of Team Canada, received a congratulatory telephone call from Prime Minister Jean Chretien. It was carried live on national TV.

Chretien: It was an awesome game and we're so proud of you. All of Canada is cheering at this moment.

Gretzky: First of all, thank you very much. All the players and the coaches deserve all the credit. They worked really hard. They put in a tremendous amount of effort and teamwork and they definitely deserved the gold medal today. It's great after 50 years to bring back the gold medal to our country where it belongs and we're very proud of our team today.

Chretien: You know Wayne, we all say in Canada that Gretzky has the golden touch.

Gretzky: (laughter) Well these guys here deserve all the credit. They worked very hard. I'm most happy for everyone on the team. I'm extremely happy for Martin Brodeur. There was a lot of controversy over that and Marty came up big at 3-2 and made some big saves. But our team just kept going and going. We definitely deserved the gold medal, we were the better team today. My hat goes off to the U.S. team, they had a great tournament.

Chretien: Great, Sakic and the goalie were fabulous and I just want to congratulate them. They were all good, so determined and such a will to win. The Canadian way. Bravo! Bravo!

Hockey Gold Unites a Country

ROBERT RUSSO
Canadian Press

WEST VALLEY CITY, Utah, Feb. 24, 2002 — The Olympic gold medal is returning to hockey's birthplace. Team Canada soared from underachiever to Olympic champion Sunday, snuffing out a half-century of thwarted Olympic hockey ambitions and sending a hockey-nuts nation into delirium.

The Canadian men thumped their American cousins, 5-2, three days after the Canadian women won gold by defeating the U.S., 3-2. Remarkably, Canada's gold came 50 years to the day after a collection of enthusiastic amateurs known as the Edmonton Mercurys won the its last Olympic championship.

As the final minute dwindled down to its final moments Sunday, both teams were serenaded with a leather-lunged version of "O Canada" from the thousands of Canadians who drove, bused or flew to watch their team end 50 years of futility at the Winter Games.

Among them were Patrick McCarthy and Jules Campeau who arrived bleary-eyed on a 6 a.m. Sunday flight from Vancouver after paying $2,750 US for a pair of tickets on EBay.

"This is our '72, this our moment" McCarthy said, referring to the Summit Series versus the Soviets. "And we have our Paul Henderson."

That would be Joe Sakic. The tournament MVP finished magnificently today with two goals and two assists.

An injury prevented Sakic from making a big impact at Nagano four years ago. That Canadian team finished a dreary fourth in 1998 and Wayne Gretzky was handed the challenge of manufacturing a squad that could snatch back Canada's game.

"It might be their only game, but they're good at it," groused Chris Chelios, captain of the U.S. team.

An enormously relieved Gretzky celebrated the final buzzer with some vigorous fist-pumping and a hug from his American wife, Janet.

"We desperately needed to win this tournament," a more subdued Gretzky said afterwards.

Canada's pursuit of the gold medal mesmerized Canadians. The CBC predicted the Sunday afternoon game would draw the largest TV audience in the nation's history — not just for sports, but for any event.

Canada staggered and stumbled into these Olympics. Tagged as the pre-tournament favourites, the world's best players looked pitiful in their first game against the Swedes and indifferent in a narrow win over the Germans.

A 3-3 tie with the Czech Republic was more promising.

Still Canadians fretted. Gretzky fumed.

The whole carefully constructed ensemble appeared to be coming unhinged after Gretzky accused the whole world of hating Canadians.

His basic message: When it comes to hockey, the world is a French figure skating judge.

It proved to be a brilliant stroke. He succeeded in shifting attention and criticism from his reeling charges onto his own aching back.

In case his message was lost, he called another news conference to reiterate what he'd said in the press conference the day before.

But with time to gel, a victory over Finland and then one brilliant stroke of good fortune — Swedish goalie Tommy Salo's inability to duck a puck fired at his cranium — Canada found itself catapulted into an easy semifinal draw against the plucky Belarussians who ousted Sweden, the class of the early going.

The Americans, who became the strongest and steadiest squad during the tournament, were forced to fend off a ferocious Russian team to reach the final.

There was the sense that this was a summit meeting of hockey talents in the current world. Americans, who make up about a quarter of all NHL players, were actually scoring slightly more goals-per-game than their Canadian counterparts before the pros took their Olympic break.

The requisite government representatives were on hand to lend the occasion the political heft needed to make it an event beyond sports.

U.S. Vice-President Dick Cheney, temporarily

Hockey fans celebrate Team Canada's 5-2 Olympic gold medal win over team USA in the streets in downtown Ottawa on Sunday, Feb. 24, 2002.

sprung from the secure undisclosed location that he's been squirrelled away in since Sept. 11, represented the Bush administration.

Canada's own deputy prime minister, John Manley, made for cross-border political balance.

On wider rinks, with no fighting allowed and a premium placed on the artistic elements of the game — skating, shooting and passing — the game played during the Olympics bore only a slight resemblance to the duller NHL game.

But this contest was not without its savagery. These same players who, in a few days, will sit beside each other in NHL dressing rooms across the continent, proved adept at stickwork both legal and illegal.

American sniper Brett Hull appeared to be trying to undress Simon Gagne by running his stick up, down and under the Canadian forward's jersey.

But there was little of the rancour that would normally flow from a feisty game.

American players, silver medals adorning their sweaters, posed for pictures with Canadian players and their golds after the match.

There was also the realization that while Canada might have reclaimed its Olympic glory, it will be a battle to stay on top.

"I don't think you'll see any country ever dominate international hockey again," said Steve Yzerman, Canada's grey-bearded wizard. "We're all too balanced now for any team to dominate. I just hope they keep using NHL players in the Olympics."

50 Years After 1952, Canada Yearns for Gold

J ust around midnight, as Friday evening blended into Saturday morning, some 40 hours before Team Canada and the U.S. team would play for the 2002 gold medal, a public television station in the Utah state capital of Salt Lake City, aired a quaint old documentary about the 1952 Olympic Winter Games in Norway. The color film was blurry with age and wear.

Most of the events on the documentary were held outdoors. The narrator's voice spoke in the style of old-fashioned newsreels.

Suddenly, among the Dick Button figure-skating clips and scenes of people on snowy hillsides drinking from steaming cups, there appeared a brief glimpse of hockey. On a rectangular rink with low sideboards, Canada was playing the U.S. for the gold medal, Without naming any players or providing many details of the tournament, the American narrator concluded in a weary tone of voice: "Finally, the hockey series was won — as it has been every time but once — by Canada."

Who was to know then that this would be Canada's last Olympic hockey gold medal, a half-century ago?

"It's been so long, we have to look at pictures to see guys that were there," said Canada's current coach, Pat Quinn.

Members of the Edmonton Waterloo Mercurys hockey team, from left, Jack Davies, Don Gauf, Bill Dawe, Monty Ford, Eric Paterson and Al Purvis pose with a picture of the hockey team in Edmonton in this Dec. 10, 2001 photo. The Mercurys were the last Canadian team to win an Olympic gold medal in ice hockey, accomplishing the feat in 1952 in Oslo, Norway.

Canada's Journey to Olympic Hockey Gold

YEAR	VENUE	GOLD	SILVER	BRONZE
1920*	Summer	Canada	—	—
1924	Chamonix, France	Canada	USA	Great Britain
1928	St. Moritx, Switzerland	Canada	Sweden	Switzerland
1932	Lake Placid, USA	Canada	USA	Germany
1936	Garmisch, Germany	Great Britain	Canada	USA
1948	St. Moritz, Switzerland	Canada	Czechoslovakia	Switzerland
1952	Oslo, Norway	Canada	USA	Sweden
1956	Cortina, Italy	Soviet Union	USA	Canada
1960	Squaw Valley, USA	USA	Canada	Soviet Union
1964	Innsbruck, Austria	Soviet Union	Sweden	Czechoslovakia
1968	Grenoble, France	Soviet Union	Czechoslovakia	Canada
1972	Sapporo, Japan	Soviet Union	USA	Czechoslovakia
1976	Innsbruck, Austria	Soviet Union	Czechoslovakia	Germany
1980	Lake Placid, USA	USA	Soviet Union	Sweden
1984	Sarajevo, Yugoslavia	Soviet Union	Czechoslovakia	Sweden
1988	Calgary, Alberta	Soviet Union	Finland	Sweden
1992	Albertville, France	Soviet Union	Canada	Finland
1994	Lillehammer, Norway	Sweden	Canada	Finland
1998	Nagano, Japan	Czech Republic	Russia	Finland
2002	Salt Lake City, USA	Canada	USA	Russia

*Contested at the Summer Olympic Games.

The Preliminaries

Say It Ain't So, Cujo!

Sweden, led by Mats Sundin, buries Canada

PAUL HUNTER
The Toronto Star

WEST VALLEY CITY, Utah, Feb. 15, 2002 — It wasn't so much that Canada lost. The real concern for a nation of anxious hockey fanatics today is that their hockey heroes also looked lost. Totally lost.

There was no magic from Mario Lemieux in his return to international hockey. No explosiveness from Paul Kariya, who has been counting the days to these Olympic Games since missing out on Nagano in 1998. No game-saving heroics from Curtis Joseph. No comprehension from a defence that struggled with the big ice and the absence of a red line. No help from the forwards in their own end.

Sweden, led by Toronto Maple Leaf captain Mats Sundin, stretched out the ice and picked Team Canada apart, 5-2.

The consolation, of course, is that this game means little in the long run. The first three games of this tournament are strictly for seeding purposes in the medal round. But the meaninglessness of this game is only valid if the Canadians use the next two games, starting tomorrow against Germany, to right themselves. And build on their too-little, too-late flurry in the third.

"We have to take this as a lesson. We got hammered," said Team Canada coach Pat Quinn. "If we don't take that lesson we'll be going home early."

Team Canada is listing now, scuttled by a variation of the Swedish Torpedo their coach Hardy Nilsson calls "big-ice hockey," and there will be much work ahead before the medal round begins, and the games become lose-and-go-home, on Wednesday.

And the players understand that they'll be working under tremendous scrutiny from back home. Defenceman Al MacInnis, asking for a little understanding from his countrymen, gave a couple of reporters a post-game speech reminiscent of Phil Esposito's plea to the nation when Canada fell behind to the Russians in the 1972 Summit Series.

"I know Canadians would like us to win all six games but sometimes that's not going to happen," MacInnis said. "Even though we lost the hockey game we still haven't lost anything yet. We know we

Game Summary

BOX SCORE

Canada	1	0	1	—	**2**
Sweden	1	4	0	—	**5**

FIRST PERIOD

1. CAN, Blake (Peca, Fleury) 02:37
2. SWE, Sundin (Alfredsson) 05:30
Penalty — SWE, Sundin (holding) 11:31.

SECOND PERIOD

3. SWE, Sundstrom (Nylander, Naslund) 6:06
4. SWE, Sundin (Alfredsson, Lidstrom) 10:42
5. SWE, K. Jonsson (Zetterberg) 11:47
6. SWE, Dahlen (Sundstrom, Sundin) 15:58 (pp)
Penalty — CAN, MacInnis (high-sticking) 15:18.

THIRD PERIOD

7. CAN, Brewer (Nolan) 15:39
Penalties — SWE, Olausson (delay of game) 0:27, SWE, Ragnarsson (tripping) 7:16.

SHOTS ON GOAL

Sweden	10	11	4	—	**25**
Canada	15	3	17	—	**35**

Goal — Sweden: Tommy Salo; Canada: Curtis Joseph.
Power-plays (goals-chances) — Sweden: 1-1; Canada 0-3.

can be a lot better and we know (the criticism) is going to start but we'll deal with it. We're grown men here. We can handle it. We're going to be stronger as this tournament goes on and that's the most important thing," MacInnis added.

"This isn't the first time a Canadian team is going to take heat and it won't be the last. There's a lot of hockey left to be played."

One of Canada's major concerns, apart from getting more from their stars, will be adapting to the big ice and the absence of a two-line offside.

After Canada jumped to a 1-0 lead, thanks to Rob Blake's early blast between the legs of Tommy Salo, the Swedes began to exploit the international rules with which they are more familiar. Using their forwards almost like wide receivers, they would break for the blue line looking for the long-bomb pass, and

Sweden's Mats Sundin (13) scores a goal against Canada's Curtis Joseph (31) during the first period.

Mario Lemieux (66) stands at center ice alone after Team Canada's 5-2 loss to Sweden.

Sweden goaltender Tommy Salo (35) covers up the puck, protecting it from Jarome Iginla (12).

several times they connected behind a flat-footed Canadian defence. Nilsson said the idea is to "create space on the ice and use it."

And use it they did.

Daniel Alfredsson launched Sundin first with a beautiful blue line-to-blue line pass that put Sundin in all alone on Toronto teammate Joseph. Sundin split the defence of Eric Brewer, who had one of Canada's goals, and MacInnis. Sundin faked a shot from the mid-slot, moved closer and buried a shot between the legs of a shaky Joseph.

The show was on. And it was impressive as yellow and blue sweaters weaved in and out of the Canadians, creating chance after chance.

"We were full of holes — Swiss cheese," huffed Quinn, the Team Canada coach.

Niklas Sundstrom, left uncovered in front by Steve Yzerman, made it 2-1 early in the second and then Sundin followed that with a slapper past Joseph's glove hand from the left faceoff circle. Former Leaf Kenny Jonsson and Ulf Dahlen, both on goals initiated by long zone-to-zone passes, pushed it to 5-1 as the Swedes scored four goals in 8:52 during a second period Kariya called "embarrassing."

"They made it look easy. They stretched it out and created 2-on-1 breaks," said Blake. "They control the puck so well.

Said Sweden's Mikael Renberg, Sundin's winger in Toronto: "I don't think Canada played its best hockey game."

Canada's Curtis Joseph (31) looks down in dismay after giving up the fourth goal to Sweden.

Sundin Becomes Cujo's Worst Nightmare

ROSIE DIMANNO
The Toronto Star

WEST VALLEY CITY, Utah, Feb. 15, 2002 — IN THE ABRUPTLY altered alliances of Olympic hockey, Mats Sundin is the enemy within.

From without, he's the fellow who scored two goals tonight against Team Canada, the catalyst behind a rude spanking inflicted on Pat Quinn's tiffany NHLers — that grand group dispatched to the XIX Winter Games in pursuit of nothing less than gold.

Or, viewed from the perspective of Toronto — centre of the hockey universe — Sundin is the quisling who employed insider information against Maple Leaf teammate Curtis Joseph, turning the latter's Olympic debut into a thing of horror.

No. 1: From in close, one-on-one after picking up a long, stringy pass from Daniel Alfredsson, Sundin bested his pal, faking a shot that lured Joseph to the right, opening his pads, then tucking the puck five-hole. Yeah, just like in practice.

No. 2: A slapper, inside the post, arguably the worst goal Joseph surrendered in Game 1, and Sundin's fifth Olympic goal, career.

Captain Sweden, not Captain Leafs.

If Joseph had forgotten what it's like to face Sundin in the heat of battle, tonight's 5-2 loss was a brisk reminder. And now he will recall how his NHL brethren feel when Sundin comes flying over the blue line in possession of the puck, or in position to take command of it.

Not that Sundin would rise to the bait of teammate-on-teammate subtext, Leaf Primo versus Leaf Supremo, and how the advantage went to the Swede against the Canadian in this particular encounter.

"I don't think it was a real advantage," claimed Sundin, stripped down to his yellow and blue Tre Kronor undergarments.

"We didn't even know who was going to play for Team Canada," he continued, reluctant to address the most compelling subplot of this game, a contest engaged less than 24 hours after most of the Canadians had even assembled in Salt Lake. Not that Sweden had any more time to prepare, although Swedish players are, by dint of origin, more familiar with the peculiarities of the international game, the bigger ice surface, the absence of the red line. Even those like Sundin who are many years removed from the hockey of their formative years, save for the occasional return engagements at Olympics and World Championships.

"I don't think playing with Curtis was a big advantage in tonight's game," Sundin insisted. But that ignores the fact he has an intimate familiarity with Joseph's tendencies, his strengths and frailties. Of course, Joseph has similar knowledge of Sundin. But, on this occasion, the edge went to the shooter. Twice.

"Once the game starts, it's (just like) you're playing another team," said Sundin. "I'm good friends with Curtis. And who knows? Maybe we'll meet again later in the tournament and he might not let one goal in. That's hockey."

Well, that's the ingrained perversity of Olympic hockey, when NHL teammates change lobsters and dance for their nations. And since the NHL married into the Olympic family four years ago, this is precisely what makes the tournament so much more fascinating.

> *"I don't think playing with Curtis (Joseph) was a big advantage in tonight's game. Once the game starts, it's (just like) you're playing another team."*
> — MATS SUNDIN

Swedish coach Hardy Nillson, for one, was delighted that the first good scoring opportunity, after Canada had taken a 1-0 lead on a goal by Rob Blake, had fallen to Sundin, who just happens to be third among goal scorers back in the you-know-what. "I was quite happy he had the first chance, because he's usually able to score."

Yet Sundin was also victimized by the lure of the long pass, the sudden reversal of play, when Sweden gambled again on freewheeling through the neutral zone. Eric Brewer broke up the pass from Alfredsson this time, going coast-to-coast to beat Tommy Salo.

"You want to have a strong forecheck and press the other team, but you also have to watch your back," said Sundin.

Of course, usually the last man back there for Sundin is Joseph.

Canada Squeaks Through Against Germany

Kariya: 'We didn't play very well, but we got the win'

PAUL HUNTER
The Toronto Star

PROVO, Utah, Feb. 17, 2002 — Yikes. Canada eked out a victory here tonight, but it will do nothing to quell anxieties at home or the nervousness that must surely be enveloping the men's Olympic hockey team.

Canada edged the Germans, 3-2, and barely avoided what could have been a humbling disaster against a country that emerged from the Olympic qualifying round.

The Canadians, while playing better and smarter than they did in Friday's embarrassing 5-2 loss to the Swedes, did nothing to grab the momentum they had hoped to carry into a crucial contest tomorrow night against the Czech Republic. The opposite might be true as the Canadians, with remade lines and revamped defensive pairings, watched a 3-0 lead in the third period crumble into the narrowest of victories.

They didn't "hammer" the Germans as team executive director Wayne Gretzky had hoped. Instead, they almost got nailed themselves against a country the Czechs demolished, 8-2, on Friday.

"Whether we win, 3-2 or 8-0, a win is a win. That's all we're worried about," defenceman Chris Pronger said. "Close doesn't count. The only thing that matters is if you lose."

But Canada certainly didn't win with style.

Facing a German team that repeatedly lined up four across the blue line, the Canucks did little to create a sustained attack.

They had chances, sometimes falling or losing the puck when they did, and needed a second-period five-minute power play to build the lead that almost slipped away.

"We didn't play very well, but we got the win. I just don't think we're in sync right now," said Paul Kariya, who potted one of the goals as Canada grabbed a 3-0 lead in the second period.

"But it's starting to come. I think we just need a few more days."

Game Summary

BOX SCORE

Canada	0	3	0	—	**3**
Germany	0	0	2	—	**2**

FIRST PERIOD

No scoring.

Penalties — CAN, Lindros (roughing) 0:24, GER Ehrhoff (cross-checking) 7:59, CAN, Pronger (high-sticking) 13:00.

SECOND PERIOD

1. CAN, Sakic (Gagn/) 8:59
2. CAN, Kariya (Nolan) 14:23 (pp)
3. CAN, Foote (Jovanovski, Nieuwendyk) 18:25

Penalties — CAN, Blake (tripping) 4:35, GER, Kunce (roughing major, game misconduct) 13:24.

THIRD PERIOD

4. GER, Lott (MacKay, Ludemann) 7:36
5. GER, Hecht (Shubert, Abstreiter) 13:51, pp

Penalties — CAN, Lindros (high-sticking) 3:19, CAN, MacInnis (tripping) 12:16.

SHOTS ON GOAL

Germany	8	4	8	—	**20**
Canada	10	17	10	—	**37**

Goal — Germany: Marc Seliger; Canada: Martin Brodeur.

Power-plays (goal-chances) — Germany: 1-5; Canada: 1-3.

So now, for Canada, it's a race against the clock. They have made some strides, such as doing a much better job moving the puck up-ice, but this squad doesn't look at all ready to challenge for a medal.

"We're making some strides, we're moving forward, but I'm sure not as fast as everyone would like," veteran forward Joe Nieuwendyk said.

Team Canada en route from the lockeroom to the ice prior to their game against Germany.

Brendan Shanahan (14) tries a wrap-around shot on Germany's goaltender, Marc Seliger (33).

Canada will have Mario Lemieux in the lineup against the Czechs after he took last night off to rest what is thought to be a hip injury.

The goaltending situation, however, remains up in the air. Martin Brodeur got the start last night over Maple Leaf Curtis Joseph, who was shaky in the loss to Sweden.

Brodeur was authoritative in his puck handling, but then allowed the two late goals.

Head coach Pat Quinn said "no decision" had been made on the goaltender for tonight and even hinted that Ed Belfour could be brought out of the stands to stand between the pipes. But that suggestion likely reflected Quinn's annoyance at being asked about his goaltending.

Brodeur, who followed in the footsteps of his father, Denis, who played goal for Canada at the 1956 Winter Games, was pleased with his performance and said

**Scott Niedermayer (27) gets checked by
Germany's Daniel Kreutzer (26).**

the victory was better than indicated by the score.

"People that watched the game (will see that)," he said. "But if you went out and had a beer and watched bobsled and you see that result, I don't think the people in Canada will be real happy about it.

"What happened? But if you watched it, you saw that we dominated the whole game and we played well at both ends of the ice. We created some chances. That's good enough."

Good enough perhaps, but it's clear this team is not yet ready to challenge for gold or a medal of any type. And the pressure is mounting.

"We're tense now and we're struggling to deal with the tenseness," Quinn said.

Kariya scored with the man advantage during that German major in the second — defenceman Daniel Kunce got five for roughing and cutting Ryan Smyth — and then Adam Foote potted another one second after the penalty expired to give Canada a 3-0 lead. But the Germans stormed back in the third with a pair of goals to put a huge scare into Canada.

Canada's Paul Kariya (9) takes a slap shot against Germany in the first period of play at the Peaks Ice Arena in Provo, Utah.

Canada Sticks to NHL Tactics

'Have to play the way we've always played,' MacInnis says

PAUL HUNTER
The Toronto Star

PROVO, Utah, Feb. 17, 2002 — The Swedes have their big-ice hockey. Tonight, the Canadians introduced little-ice hockey.

Or, more accurately, reintroduced it.

After being embarrassed, 5-2, in their opening Olympic contest against Sweden, the Canucks went into tonight's game against Germany planning to play their own game, the game they brought with them from the NHL.

Offensively, they're going to play as if the red line is still there. While that would seem to be taking a weapon out of their hands, one that all the other nations seem fully prepared to exploit, they feel as if they have to play a game with which they are more familiar.

They felt that in the opener they played into the hands of the splendid Swedes by trying to take advantage of the absence of a red line and look too often for the long-bomb pass. The result, the Canadians felt, was that they were spread out too far on the ice. Forwards ended up hovering near the opposition blue line, taking away any targets for the defence to pass to. There was no support for the puck as the defencemen had to face the two-man Swedish forecheck on their own.

The result was a disaster, with the Canadians spread out so far on the ice that the Swedes were able to pick them apart, finding easy passing lanes to spring players for chances on net.

Even though the outcome of last night's game was almost embarrassing for the Canadians, they often moved the puck smartly through neutral ice and then, when faced with the Germans lined up across the blue line, resorted to the NHL tactic of dumping the puck deep and chasing it.

"The other night against Sweden we were way

Team Canada's Al MacInnis (2) controls the puck against Germany.

> *"When we spread out like that it's playing right into their hands. We have to play the way we've always played and not worry about the long pass and not worry about the lack of a red line . . . With the players we've got, we've got plenty of speed and if we stick to our so-called North American game, we'll be fine."*
>
> — **AL MACINNIS**

ahead of the play and we had our backs to the defencemen all night," said centre Mike Peca. "Tonight we did a better job staying together through the neutral zone. It took us a period to finally find it."

Against Sweden, in contrast, the Canadians looked both lost and confused on the big ice.

"When we spread out like that it's playing right into their hands," defenceman Al MacInnis said before last night's game. "We have to play the way we've always played and not worry about the long pass and not worry about the lack of a red line. We have to focus on supporting the puck coming out of our end with speed through the neutral zone. With the players we've got, we've got plenty of speed and if we stick to our so-called North American game, we'll be fine."

But doesn't this simply put Canada at a disadvantage on the big ice surface if they are not willing to take advantage of a rule that is available to them to create offence?

"I don't think so," said Peca. "You look at the guys in our lineup who have had success with the red line there and there's no reason to say that if we continue that same way we can't continue to have that same success."

Canada Wins Pride Back

A 3-3 tie with Czech Republic restores some confidence

PAUL HUNTER
The Toronto Star

WEST VALLEY CITY, Utah, Feb. 18, 2002 — Two significant ingredients returned to Team Canada tonight: Passion and Mario Lemieux.

Whether the former would have existed without the latter is impossible to say but the combination, one that injected some much-needed confidence into the men's team, earned Team Canada a 3-3 tie with the Czech Republic and should give Canada some momentum in its push for a medal.

It might even, at least for the moment, quiet some of the anxiety at home.

"Tonight we had a lot of intensity," Lemieux said afterwards. "That's the way we have to play from now on."

Indeed against defending Olympic champs, Team Canada hit the ice with a desire and cohesiveness that had been missing in its first two games. There was a commitment to taking the body, there were smart passes through the neutral zone and there were game-saving stops from Martin Brodeur.

But, more than anything, there was Lemieux.

The big captain had sat out Sunday's 3-2 win over Germany with a hip injury and he might as well have missed Friday's 5-2 loss to Sweden, such was the level of his ineffectiveness. But, with the stage set for his return and a nation braced to begin the obits on the death of Canadian hockey, Lemieux responded with two goals and the kind of on-ice leadership this squad desperately lacked.

"To have one of the greatest players ever lace up his skates, it helped us offensively, defensively and with our confidence," said his linemate Paul Kariya.

And if Lemieux helped generate a perfect tie this was it. A win would have moved Canada into second place in Group C of the Olympic draw and that would have meant a matchup against the highly skilled Russians when the games become lose-and-go-home. Instead, Canada gained the respect of playing even with a skilled Czech squad while still retaining its third-place seeding. That means Canada will play Finland — with a good chance to move on in the Tournament.

"We feel we're back in this now," said Joe Nieuwendyk, whose goal with less than four minutes remaining earned the tie. "Little by little, we're playing better and better."

The game against Finland will be at 10:15 p.m. EST on Wednesday. If Canada does advance past

Paul Kariya, left, watches as Czech Republic goalie Dominik Hasek, right, holds the puck in his glove as he falls in his net after a shot by Mario Lemieux during the second period. After review of the play Lemieux was awarded the goal. The game ended in a 3-3 tie.

Game Summary

BOX SCORE

Canada	1	1	1	—	**3**
Czech Republic	1	1	1	—	**3**

FIRST PERIOD

1. CAN, Lemieux (Niedermayer) 9:11
2. CZE, Havlat (Jagr) 18:23

Penalties — CAN, MacInnis (hooking) 6:12, CZE, Dopita (hooking) 15:29, CAN, Foote (slashing) 19:51.

SECOND PERIOD

3. CZE, Havlat (Kubina) 3:08
4. CAN, Lemieux (Yzerman) 18:49

Penalties — CZE, Kaberle (holding) 5:22, CZE, Rucinsky (hooking) 12:23.

THIRD PERIOD

5. CZE, Dopita (Hamrlik) 13:17
6. CAN, Nieuwendyk (Fleury) 16:36

Penalties — None.

SHOTS ON GOAL

Czech Rep	6	7	16	—	**29**
Canada	13	15	8	—	**36**

Goal — Czech Republic: Dominique Hasek; Canada: Martin Brodeur.
Power-plays (goals-chances) — Czech Republic: 0-2; Canada: 0-3.

Finland, it would then play the winner of Sweden against Belarus.

Lemieux's return, not only to the ice but to form, changes the complexion of this tournament and gives Canada the skilled offensive general it lacked in the first two outings.

Lemieux, back playing at centre tonight, had wanted to return against the Germans but at the urging of Wayne Gretzky, the team's executive director, he sat out. In hindsight it was the right call.

Canada won without him Sunday and tonight. Lemieux looked energized and excited. He could have had a couple more goals but his shots went wide.

"We did a lot of treatments in the last few days and I felt better," he said. "Any day you can have off at this time of the season is refreshing. I just felt great from the start. I was able to skate a little better because I was at centre, getting some speed, supporting the play a little more, so I felt more comfortable than just standing still most of the time."

Lemieux's first goal was a terrific individual effort as he knocked down a long Scott Niedermayer pass at centre, cruised down the left wing and beat Dominik Hasek through the five-hole.

Lemieux's second required some help from the video replay judge. On a 2-on-1 with Kariya, Lemieux fired the shot that Hasek snared with his glove hand but Hasek fell back into the net and the goal counted.

"I thought it was in. Dominik's whole body was over the line," said Lemieux, who tied the game at 2-2 in the second. "The only thing I was afraid of was that they could not see the puck from above."

Defenceman Al MacInnis said the tie changes the atmosphere around the club.

"That was the kind of effort we needed, that's for sure," said MacInnis.

"Not only to bolster the confidence of the team but also so we realize we're capable of playing this well. There was a lot of second-guessing as to whether we were ever going to step forward."

Czech Republic's Radek Dvorak (19), left, takes a shot on goal against Canada's goalkeeper Martin Brodeur (3). Adam Foote, 2nd right, looks on in the first period.

Cujo Banished to the Doghouse

Leaf star sits in the stands for Czech game; he may not play

PAUL HUNTER
The Toronto Star

WEST VALLEY CITY, Utah, Feb. 18, 2002 — In three days, Curtis Joseph has gone from being Team Canada's No.1 goaltender to street clothes, sitting in the stands tonight as he did throughout the 1998 Olympics at Nagano.

Whether Joseph's banishment to spectator status is permanent is unclear, but Martin Brodeur said he is preparing as if he is going to be the starter in Canada's quarter-final game against Finland late tomorrow night.

The change in goaltending assignments for tonight's game against the Czech Republic was a shocker. Ed Belfour, who spent the first two games in the stands as the third-stringer, was dressed on the bench as the backup.

"We haven't eliminated any of the three," coach Pat Quinn said after Team Canada tied the Czechs, 3-3. "They're all good goalies. Marty has had two pretty good games now. But to say any one of them is not going to play would not be right."

Based on tonight's performance, the starting job should be Brodeur's to lose and that's how the New Jersey netminder is approaching it.

"My first goal was to play in the Olympics and then, after that, to carry the torch all the way to the end," said Brodeur. "In my mind, I'm going to start against the Finns unless they say otherwise. That's how I'm going to prepare myself."

Wayne Gretzky, executive director of Team Canada, described Brodeur's performance as "tremendous."

Midway through the second period, he made a spectacular diving save on a Jan Hrdina shot that appeared to be going into an empty net. Moments later he made an excellent shoulder stop on a Jiri Dopita blast. He also exuded confidence and control all night, unlike Joseph, who appeared to be fighting the puck in Canada's tournament-opening 5-2 loss to Sweden. Brodeur is also the NHL's best puckhandler among goaltenders and that skill is a definite asset on the big ice.

Joseph did not make himself available to reporters after the game but how being bounced out of uniform by Quinn, who is also his coach with the Maple Leafs, will affect their relationship in Toronto will be fascinating to watch. Joseph also becomes an unrestricted free agent at season's end.

"It's a situation we all knew coming in," said Brodeur. "We knew the job was up for grabs for anybody. Who knows what's going to happen? I don't know for sure that someone else won't get some ice time yet."

Even if Brodeur starts the next game, Joseph and Belfour could again switch places. Brodeur said he thought getting Belfour out of the stands for at least one game was planned all along. Brodeur said Quinn asked him before the tournament started whether he would be willing to sit in the stands for a game if Joseph was playing the majority of the games. "He asked me if I would mind if Eddie came down as the backup one game. I said, 'I wouldn't mind,' " recounted Brodeur.

"I was on the bench every game in Nagano and Curtis was in the stands. I'm sure he would have loved to come down and be part of it, to feel the ambience and to see what's going on in the locker room."

Belfour was indeed thrilled to feel more a part of the team and to get a front-row seat last night.

"Even just to be helpful in a small way is special," said Belfour, the Dallas goaltender who has handled his status with class.

"To help this team be successful is a dream come true."

Czeck Republic's Martin Havlat is congratulated by teammates (left to right) Jaromir Jagr, Roman Hamrlik and Robert Lang, for his goal against Canada's goalie Martin Brodeur, left, during first period of hockey competition.

*"It's a situation we all knew coming in.
We knew the job was up for grabs for anybody.
Who knows what's going to happen?
I don't know for sure that someone else won't get some ice time yet."*
— MARTIN BRODEUR

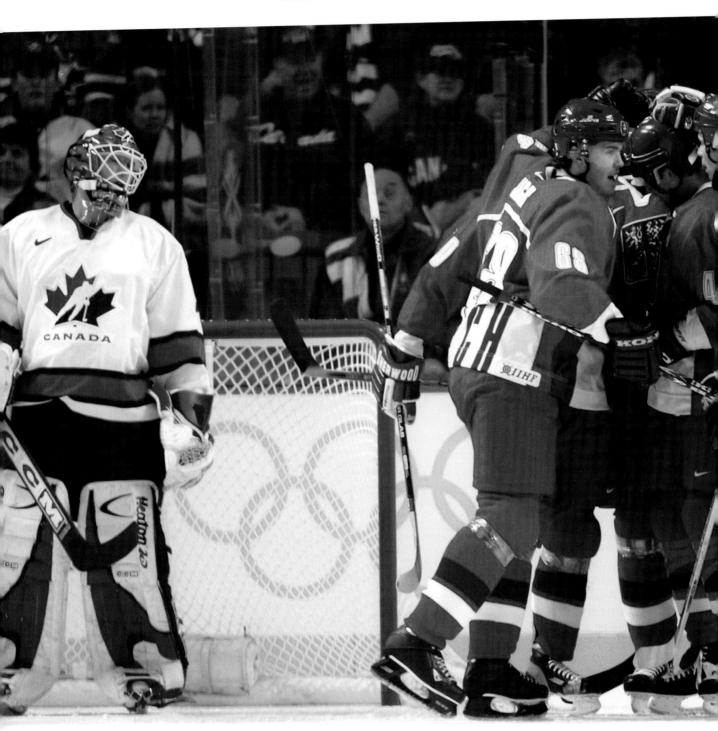

Fire-breathing Gretzky Circles the Wagons

Damien Cox
The Toronto Star

WEST VALLEY CITY, Utah, Feb. 18, 2002 — FINALLY, SOME passion. The World's Greatest Hockey Tournament, Part II, is now heading into the do-or-die phase, and Canada officially entered the fray today with its best performance to date and with a most unlikely Canadian breathing fire.

In a post-game diatribe that shocked long-time Wayne Gretzky observers, The Great One came out swinging with uncharacteristically bitter invective after a thrilling 3-3 tie with the Czech Republic tonight, accusing the hockey world of wanting to see Canada fail and "American propaganda" of trying to unsettle the Canadian Olympic team.

"I don't think we dislike the other countries as much as they hate us," said an angry Gretzky, who lives in the U.S. and owns part of the Phoenix Coyotes. "They hate us. They want to see us fail. That's what they say to us on the ice.

"Well, we've got to get the same feeling towards them."

Clearly, Gretzky and those who have put this Canadian team together have worked over the last few days to instil a siege mentality in the Team Canada dressing room, using criticism at home and the supposedly anti-Canadian sentiments of other countries to build an us-against-them attitude.

Some of that is clearly sports psychology babble, or the kind of stuff Gretzky's mentor, Glen Sather, always spouts at pivotal moments. But Gretzky was also genuinely incensed today by an incident late in the game in which Canadian forward Theo Fleury

Canadian hockey fan Michel Perreault of Ottawa cheers as Canada's hockey team takes to the ice for warm-up prior to their game against the Czech Republic.

was clearly speared twice by Czech defenceman Martin Skoula as he lay in the Czech crease area.

As soon as Fleury got to his feet, he was viciously cross-checked from behind by Roman Hamrlik.

"If that was a Canadian, it would have been the first question I would have been asked, and I want to know why nobody is asking me," said Gretzky. "Those guys should be kicked out of the tournament. If a Canadian had done that, we would be called hooligans.

"They couldn't skate with us. We skated them into the ground in the third and they should have had four or five penalties and two or three suspensions.

"Am I hot? Yeah, I am. I'm tired of people taking shots at Canada."

The Gretzky rant didn't end there.

Gretzky, in an unusually hostile mood, predicted Czech players that got away with alleged offences in tonight's game, including a blind hit by Pavel Kubina on Joe Nieuwendyk after the Dallas forward tied the game late, will face retribution when the NHL season resumes.

"Those guys will have to answer the bell, and it won't be pretty. I wouldn't want to be in that Ranger-Islander game next week," he said, a not-so-subtle suggestion Fleury will be out looking for Hamrlik.

Gretzky also vaguely targeted American media outlets for spreading unspecified false stories about Team Canada, possibly involving some veteran players being unhappy with Pat Quinn's coaching.

"(The Americans) love us not doing well," said Gretzky.

"Now there are two Canadian stories, the figure skaters (Jamie Salé and David Pelletier) and the hockey team. It's all such crap. Nobody wants us to

Wayne Gretzky, left, executive director of team Canada, and other team officials, from left, Mike Pelino, Kevin Lowe, and Bob Nicholson follow the action on the ice as their team trails the Czechs.

win but our own players.

"Well, we're still here, and we're still standing."

It didn't all make sense, but it sure was entertaining. Clearly, Gretzky and Quinn have been feeding these types of messages into the Canadian dressing room in a desperate effort to get this team angry at someone.

"We're trying to shortcut the team-building thing," acknowledged Quinn.

Winger Brendan Shanahan suggested similar strategy when asked how he felt about Canada having ceded the role of Olympic favourite to Sweden and the Americans.

"Most of the experts are picking other teams now, and that's okay. Within our dressing room we've been building something in the last few days," said Shanahan. "People are forgetting about us."

Gretzky's post-game comments were the talk of the tournament, but whether that will have lasting impact is unclear. What is clear, is that Canada found some answers to some, if not all, of it's internal questions tonight.

Mario Lemieux played centre between Paul Kariya and Steve Yzerman and scored twice, while the line of Simon Gagne-Joe Sakic-Jarome Iginla stayed intact

from the victory over Germany on Sunday.

Martin Brodeur was solid in the Canadian goal, making several excellent third-period stops, and will face Finland in the quarterfinals tomorrow.

Ed Jovanovski, meanwhile, has won the sixth defenceman's job away from Eric Brewer, who gave away the puck on the Czech Republic's second goal.

There is concern in two areas. The line of Lindros between Ryan Smyth and Owen Nolan forechecked well and created chances, but made a series of mistakes in the Canadian zone. And the defence pairing of Chris Pronger and Al MacInnis has been inconsistent.

A 1-1-1 finish in the round robin now gives Canada the task of having to beat three quality teams to win gold, while Sweden and the U.S. only have to beat two of the top hockey powers to emerge on top.

Finland will be tough on Wednesday, but should Canada get past Teemu Selanne & Co., a fascinating semifinal collision with Mats Sundin and the Swedes would likely take place.

All Gretzky has to do now, then, is figure a way to create a wave of anti-Scandinavian fervour in the Canadian dressing room to create an opportunity to fight for gold on Sunday.

The Tournament

SALT LAKE 2002

Team Canada Skins Finns

Yzerman nets winner in nerve-wracking 2-1 quarter-final victory

PAUL HUNTER
The Toronto Star

WEST VALLEY CITY, Utah, Feb. 20, 2002 — It wasn't supposed to be this nerve-wracking. It shouldn't have been this close.

Team Canada, in position to follow a golden path to the Olympic championship, almost squandered it tonight. Battling both the Finns and their own inability to finish, the Canadians frittered away several early scoring chances before hanging on for a 2-1 victory in what was a dramatic battle of wills.

The win, nail-biter that it was, puts Canada into a semifinal game against Belarus on Friday.

That's not a misprint. Earlier in the day, Belarus stunned Sweden in a 4-3 upset, a turn of events that means only the smallest of hurdles — Belarus went winless in the round robin — prevents Canada from reaching Sunday afternoon's gold-medal final. The United States and Russia will play in the other semifinal.

"I guess all the pharmacies in Canada will have to close now," Canadian forward Theo Fleury said of the national upset that is easing as this group of players starts looking more and more like a team.

"We knew it would be difficult," said captain Mario Lemieux. "All these teams here didn't come here to finish second. We've made progress every day and we're looking pretty good right now.

Theo Fleury (74) leaps above the ice in front of the goal as Finland goalie Jani Hurme (35) protects the goal and Janne Niinimaa (44) looks on.

"We need the support of all Canadians to stand behind us and to help us win the gold medal and achieve our goal. That's what we need right now."

Lemieux said the team watched the Belarus-Sweden game earlier in the day and that it was "big relief" when Belarus won and eliminated the Swedes.

"When they scored, it was pretty nice," Lemieux said.

Canadian forward Jarome Iginla cautioned against becoming complacent about Belarus.

"They seem in sync and after beating Sweden, their confidence has to be high and they will be fired up," he said.

The closeness of last night's game wasn't due to a lack of trying on Canada's part and certainly not because of a lack of skill. They created great scoring chances throughout the game but couldn't put away the pesky Finns, who had beaten them for the bronze medal four years ago at Nagano.

Joe Sakic, who opened the scoring in the first, clinked the puck off the crossbar with less than nine minutes remaining. Then a nation held its collective breath as the Canadians desperately killed the clock.

"It was a battle. They never quit," said centre Joe Nieuwendyk. "They play a style where they just keep coming at you and they did tonight. The first half of the game was real solid for us but there was no quit in that team."

The Canadians played the final period without Eric Lindros, who came into this game battling a shoulder injury and reinjured it in the second period. Defenceman Chris Pronger also had a rough night, slamming his head into the glass twice in the third period, once during a collision with Janne Niinimaa and then, again, when Teemu Selanne took him out, cutting him badly across the forehead.

Steve Yzerman, a player whose health was in question coming into this tournament because of knee surgery, had Canada's other goal, the winner, late in the second. Niklas Hagman scored for Finland.

"Maybe the big guy upstairs is on our side this time," said Fleury.

But Al MacInnis said Canada can't let up now. It has to keep getting better as a team even to ensure it gets past Belarus.

"Anything less than a gold and a lot of people will be disappointed," he said.

Sakic scored early, at the 3:00 mark. He worked a pretty give-and-go with linemate Simon Gagne and took a pass from the young Flyers winger as he cut to the net. With his incredible set of fans, Sakic con-

Game Summary

BOX SCORE

Canada	1	1	0	—	**2**
Finland	0	1	0	—	**1**

FIRST PERIOD
1. CAN, Sakic (Gagne) 3:00
Penalties — None.

SECOND PERIOD
2. CAN, Yzerman (Lemieux) 15:49
3. FIN, Hagman (Kallio, Jokinen) 16:09
Penalty — FIN, Selanne (interference) 5:52.

THIRD PERIOD
No scoring.
Penalty — CAN, Jovanovski, (boarding) 6:10.

SHOTS ON GOAL

Finland	5	8	6	—	19
Canada	15	14	5	—	34

Goal — Finland: Jani Hurme; Canada: Martin Brodeur.
Power-plays (goals-chances) Finland: 0-1; Canada: 0-1.

trolled the puck and ripped a backhander between the legs of Finnish goalie Jani Hurme.

For the next 30 minutes, the Canadians did everything right but couldn't score. Through the first 40 minutes, they held a 29-13 advantage but only a one-goal lead. After seeing that monstrous upset earlier in the day when Belarus took out Sweden, collars must have been getting tight in the perch at centre ice where executive director Wayne Gretzky was watching the game with the Team Canada hierarchy.

Finally, at 15:49 of the second, some of that spectacular Canadian puckhandling paid off and it was two of the grand masters of the game who combined on the goal. Pushing into the offensive zone, Yzerman fired the puck to Lemieux in the high slot and drifted down the left side. As if they'd been together for years, Lemieux feathered a perfect pass back to Yzerman, who ripped the puck into the open side past Hurme to make it 2-0.

Breathing room, right? Not quite.

A mere 20 seconds after Yzerman's goal, Hagman scored to make it 2-1.

Mario Lemiuex (66) of Canada tries to fend off Finland's Tomi Kallio (17) and Olli Jokinen (12) as they battle for control of the puck during first period action.

Team Canada Survives, Barely

ROSIE DIMANNO
The Toronto Star

WEST VALLEY CITY, Utah, Feb. 20, 2002 — Breathless hockey. Gasping, panting, heart-in-your-throat hockey.

Whatever-it-takes kind of hockey, on a rainy night in Salt Lake, at the end of a befuddling day when all preconceived notions about the Olympic shinny tournament went out the window.

Out go the Swedes. Out go the Czechs.

Out, finally, went the Finns. And on went Team Canada.

The Canadians reacted to the drop of the puck like a bunch of junkyard dogs pouncing on raw meat. They growled, they clawed, they slavered. There were intense battles along the boards, vicious confrontations in the corners, and assaults in the first degree in front of the net.

Fourteen shots they pumped at Jani Hurme in the first period, holding the Finns to a paltry five-spot against Martin Brodeur, taking away the lanes, laying on the body, none so robustly as Rob Blake, who had his best game of the tournament.

Yet for all their efforts, they had only one goal to show for it, which felt ominous and foreboding — so many opportunities, not squandered, but simply thwarted by a netminder who remained unrattled. And there are so many illustrative tales, cautionary tales, in hockey lore of insignificant netminders playing out of their minds on one particular night and forever changing the course of history.

Canada's goalie Martin Brodeur (30) loses his mask while protecting the goal, as teammate Paul Kariya (9) goes sprawling behind him during the third period.

Could Hurme be one of them, on more accursed David to Canada's Goliath?

It was Joe Sakic who solved him first, early and cleverly, a backhander through Hurme's legs after taking a pass from Simon Gagne, just three minutes into the first period.

So it stood, for the longest time, even though Team Canada gave the impression of being just on the cusp of breaking out with an offensive barrage, the scoring fireworks of which they are so eminently capable — and which just hadn't been seen in Salt Lake.

Obstinately, effectively, the Finns continued to contain the Canadians. Maddeningly, despite the larger dimensions of the rink, there seemed to be even less time and space for the Canadian forwards to orchestrate the plays they wanted.

When they did, Hurme proved efficient to the challenge — most particularly a huge first period save off Brendan Shanahan. Unfortuantely, Shanahan couldn't get it up quite far enough, from the corner of the net. Hurme was on his back, likely had no idea where the puck was, when he managed to stop it with his leg, just kicking up and back, a Hail Mary save.

Even with a one-man advantage, Teemu Selanne in the box for interfering — he'd pushed Al MacInnis into Brodeur and Brodeur inside his cage; the Canadians could not make life easier for themselves. There were great big booming shots, monstrous shots, from the point, as if the Canucks wanted to drive that puck right through the boards. What they couldn't manage was to get the shot on net.

Too tight, too close.

Only for 20 seconds did the Canadians give themselves some breathing space. That was the duration of their two-goal lead, established when Steve Yzerman went tic-tac-toe with Mario Lemieux, then shot at an extreme angle.

But the cheering had barely stopped before Finland got one back at the other end, Niklas Hagman beating Brodeur.

Then it got scary again, the Finns seemingly more adept at the long pass, immediately wheeling and churning when it possession of the puck. More work for Brodeur than he'd experienced through the first 20 minutes.

Sakic hit the crossbar, with about 10 minutes left in the third and it appeared that Team Canada was blowing its chances.

Yet Brodeur came to the rescue. Ultimately, and finally, 2-1 proved to be enough. Squeaky, nerve-wracking, but enough.

Four years ago, everything came too easy to Team Canada. They encountered little resistance in the first round. It was with a sense of entitlement that the team proceeded into the medal round, unduly concerned even about the prospect of facing Dominik Hasek in the penultimate game against the Czech Republic. After all, they had Patrick Roy guarding their flank, and that seemed a goaltending saw-off.

Alas, it did come to that, in the poisonous environment of a shootout, with the score knotted 1-1. Stung by the rattle of one Robert Reichel, and who saw that coming? With Wayne Gretzky watching glumly from the bench.

In Salt Lake City, however — and not by design, far from it — Team Canada established its merit in incremental steps, and in reverse order. From a humbling 5-2 opening loss to Sweden, through an unimpressive 3-2 victory over Germany, and a hard-fought 3-3 tie against Hasek and his Czechs.

Right: Finland's Ossi Vaananen (6), left, tumbles on the ice with Canada's Mike Peca (37) during first period.

Opposite page: Canada's Theo Fleury (74) collides with Jarkko Ruutu (37) of Finland on the boards during the first period.

Joseph Puts Team Canada Before Himself

Demoted Leaf doesn't utter negative word

PAUL HUNTER
The Toronto Star

WEST VALLEY CITY, Utah, Feb. 20, 2002 — Martin Brodeur felt like he'd been through a war. But he doesn't want to start one.

When asked about Wayne Gretzky's comments this week, that other countries hate Canada, he said he didn't think it made much of a difference.

"We're not here to make war with other countries. We're here to win a gold medal," he said. "But the support from the organization is important to us and it showed in his comments."

On the ice, the 2-1 victory over Finland was a battle. Brodeur said he was feeling it after the game.

"It's a little tougher when it's a gritty game because you're looking for the puck all the time. Guys are diving. People are crashing the net. It's harder for a goalie to look through screens all the time and physically it's a little more draining. But that's how we have to play."

Brodeur's third straight solid game further cemented Curtis Joseph, the Maple Leafs' goaltender, as the backup. But Joseph refused to let his status turn into anything negative.

"It's game day and I don't want to talk about it," said Joseph as he came off the ice after the team's morning skate. "You never know what can happen. I don't want to start talking negative on game day, to be honest with you. Ask me about anything else."

While Joseph didn't want to discuss his disappointment about losing his No. 1 designation, Gretzky praised the netminder for handling the situation professionally.

"We want everyone to stay as close knit as we can. When Eddie (Belfour) didn't play the first game and was in the stands, he was outstanding in the room and talking to the players and Curtis was the same way the other day," said Gretzky.

In his official observer status, Joseph said he has noticed Team Canada is getting stronger as it gets accustomed to the ice and pace of the games.

"It's more positive. Guys are feeling better about the big ice about their game and about each other. It's really a building process. And I think we are getting better as the tournament goes on so that's a positive thing," he said.

"Losing to Sweden in the first game was hard to take, obviously. I guess you look at the glass half full, to see that type of game as the first game rather than the fourth game."

As the team comes together, Brodeur said he's noticed his teammates are adapting to his habit of wandering from his net to fire the puck up ice.

"Every time I grab the puck guys aren't used to it, so they're coming towards me. Then I'm kind of stuck with the puck looking at everybody. It's weird but it's normal. This is not the team I've played with the last nine years. Hopefully, we'll get better as we go along."

After Win Over Belarus Stage Set for Hockey Classic

Canada faces U.S. for chance to end 50-year title drought

DAMIEN COX
The Toronto Star

WEST VALLEY CITY, Utah, Feb. 22, 2002 — Both Canada and the United States have a guaranteed Olympic silver medal in men's hockey that neither country wants.

Both, you must understand, desire only the gleam of gold.

Following in the footsteps of their respective national women's teams, the Canadians and Americans will duel for the title of Olympic men's champions tomorrow, a television bonanza-in-the-making that NHL execs desperately wanted four years ago in Japan and have now received in the land of Mormons, mountains and Jell-O.

The New York-New Jersey area will supply the goaltenders, Martin Brodeur and Mike Richter, and two of the most famous hockey icons in each country, Canada's Wayne Gretzky and Team U.S.A.'s Herb Brooks, will finally get to see whether more than a year of careful, hopeful planning will produce the desired result.

The drama is delicious, the stage unique and compelling. The result will deliver four years of analysis and discussion, more if this turns out to be the last Winter Olympics featuring teams of NHL players.

"This means a whole lot to the whole country," said Team Canada captain Mario Lemieux after he and his teammates pounded overmatched Belarus, 7-1.

"We are proud Canadians. Hockey is our sport back home. Everybody plays and loves to watch it. For us to have the chance right now to do something special for our country is something we can all cherish for a long time if we win a gold medal."

Canada, which lost gold medal Olympic games twice in the 1990's, is looking for its first gold in men's hockey since 1952.

"I don't think there will be one person on the street anywhere in Canada (tomorrow) after-

Game Summary

BOX SCORE

Canada	2	2	3	—	**7**
Belarus	1	0	0	—	**1**

FIRST PERIOD
1. CAN, Yzerman (Sakic, Blake) 6:05
2. BLR, Salei 13:24
3. CAN, Brewer (Yzerman, Sakic) 17:25
Penalties — BLR, Kopat (high-sticking) 1:52, BLR, Mikulchuk (roughing) 16:06, CAN, Fleury (roughing) 16:06.

SECOND PERIOD
4. CAN, Niedermayer (Lemieux, Kariya) 2:09 (pp)
5. CAN, Kariya (Yzerman/Lemieux) 13:28
Penalties — BLR, Kovalev (holding) 1:11, CAN, Jovanovski (tripping) 2:38, CAN, Peca (cross-checking) 5:12, BLR, Mikulchuk (boarding) 9:59.

THIRD PERIOD
6. CAN, Gagn/ (Peca) 5:21 (sh)
7. CAN, Lindros (Smyth, Nolan) 12:24 (pp)
8. CAN, Iginla (Shanahan) 16:16
Penalties — CAN Niedermayer (high-sticking) 3:31, CAN Fleury (hooking) 6:56, CAN Nolan (roughing) 8:43, BLR Team (too many men) 10:52, BLR Tsyplakov (roughing) 17:43, CAN Lindros (slashing) 17:43, CAN Lindros (unsportsmanlike conduct) 19:54.

SHOTS ON GOALS

Belarus	3	6	5	—	14
Canada	17	15	19	—	51

Goal — Belarus: Andrei Mezin (L, 1-4-0), Sergei Shabanov; Canada: Martin Brodeur (W, 3-0-1).
Power-plays (goals-chances) — Belarus: 0-5, Canada: 2-3.

Canada's Paul Kariya (9), left, Steve Yzerman, center, and Mario Lemieux celebrate Yzerman's second-period goal.

noon," predicted American forward Jeremy Roenick.

These two countries last met for an international title at the 1996 World Cup, with the Americans coming out on top.

"Wayne Gretzky has put together a diversified hockey club," said Brooks, the architect of the famous Miracle on Ice victory at the Lake Placid Olympics in 1980.

"We know them, they know us. There are no secrets in this one."

Canada beat the U.S. by one goal in the women's final last night. In a similar scenario to that game, the male version of Team Canada will try to upset an unbeaten American squad tomorrow, a team that has allowed only five goals in five Olympic contests and is seeking to reproduce the home-ice victories of the 1960 Winter Olympics in Squaw Valley, Calif., and Lake Placid.

Brodeur, who stole Curtis Joseph's starting job with Team Canada, will try to win the Olympic gold that eluded his father, Denis, when he represented Canada at the 1956 Games in Cortina d'Ampezzo, Italy, and came home with bronze.

"I wouldn't trade this life experience for anything," said Brodeur. "I will remember this for the rest of my life, just as my dad did in '56."

Two members of the Canadian side, winger Paul Kariya and Eric Lindros, have previously played in Olympic gold-medal games. Both were on the losing end, Lindros in a '92 defeat to the Unified Team, a collection of ex-Soviet republics, and Kariya in the '94 shootout defeat in Lillehammer to Sweden in which he was the last Canadian to try and fail against Tommy Salo.

"It's nice to get another shot at it," said Lindros. "You never know what's going to happen at the Olympics. Weird things occur. Who would have thought we would play Belarus in the semifinals?

"The other thing is it happens so quickly. It's an interesting tournament."

While the Americans started the tournament with a one-side shutout win over Finland and have soared throughout the competition, Canada lost its opener to Sweden by three goals and has gradually gathered a head of steam.

"We've only been here a week, but a lot of things have changed," said Steve Yzerman. "We have 100 per cent more confidence on the ice. We've

Canada's Eric Brewer (3) collides with Andrei Kovalev (13) of Belarus during second period action of their semifinal match.

learned a lot in a week."

It was the patience and intelligence of the Canadian team that stood out today in the rout over Belarus.

Canadian teams in other years have gone into international encounters with superior talent, but often that has resulted in frenetic, over-aggressive play that has led to penalties, mistakes and lapses in defensive coverage.

But not today.

Even knowing that Belarus had eliminated Sweden in an enormous upset, the Canadians had to know in their hearts that this was not an opponent that could defeat them. But instead of looking for goals and playing individually, Team Canada was, if anything, more cohesive and unselfish than in any of their prior four matches.

The 51-shot attack included offence from every line, and four players who had not previously scored in the tournament — Jarome Iginla, Scott Niedermayer, Simon Gagne and Lindros — found the net.

"The first thing was we didn't want to give them anything," said Yzerman. "We didn't want to trade chances and get sloppy.

"This is much more of a patient game than the NHL, and we're getting a lot better at that as a team instead of going full speed all the time."

The Americans have been the best team in the tournament, while the Canadians have fought through more adversity.

Richter has been utterly brilliant, stopping 19 shots from the Russians in the third period today, while Brodeur hasn't yet had to be.

Brooks' first thought on Team Canada in his post-game press conference today was the decisive impact Lemieux might have on the final.

Millions of Canadians are desperately hoping that will be the case.

Team Canada forward Eric Lindros (88), top, sends Belarus defenseman Vladimir Kopat (30) crashing to the ice during the first period of their semifinal men's hockey game.

Defence Proving to be Best Offence

Canadian blueliners jump into the action with good results

PAUL HUNTER
The Toronto Star

WEST VALLEY CITY, Utah, Feb. 22, 2002 — When Canada takes on the United States on Sunday in a cross-border battle for Olympic gold, some of the most important offence may end up coming from the defence.

The Americans have some excellent puck-moving defencemen in Brian Leetch, Brian Rafalski and a rejuvenated Phil Housley, who scored a goal yesterday while pinching from the blue line. And, now, as the Canadians become more comfortable on the big ice and less panicked about defending against long bomb passes, their blue liners are jumping into the play with more regularity. And production from the blue line has become an important part of Canada's attack.

In their 7-1 win over Belarus today, Canada got goals from Eric Brewer and Scott Niedermayer. Of their 17 goals in the tournament, five have come from defencemen.

"We've been moving the puck more and feeling a lot better moving the puck," said Vancouver defenceman Ed Jovanovski. "A lot of the guys are starting to jump up into the play and they're trying to add a dimension up front. With more ice here, you have to take what they give you. It's great for defencemen to have that much room to skate around."

Niedermayer said getting the defencemen involved offensively was something that's been stressed by the coaching staff since the team's orientation camp in September.

"I think the coaches realized that's how the game was going to evolve. They stressed it then and they stressed it again when we got here. They said it was important for that fourth guy to jump in to the play and it will often be that guy that gets the opportunity," said Niedermayer, who is a strong enough skater that he can make a foray into the offensive zone but still be one of the first back if the play turns the other way.

"Sometimes things get spread out with the big ice surface. That gives you an extra second to make your play."

That the defence is taking more and more chances says two very important things about how Team Canada has evolved since that 5-2 loss to Sweden in its opening game here.

Though they got their only goals from blueliners that night, most of the time the defencemen seemed afraid to venture too far out of their own zone out of fear they'd get beat with one of those long passes the lack of a red line allows. They also focused much of their offensive energies trying to complete one of those two-line passes themselves.

Also, there is a growing trust among the Canadians as they become more of a team on the ice. The defencemen have come to believe that if they take a chance, one of the forwards will hustle back to cover for them. It also helps that this group of Canadians is highly skilled and less prone to turn the puck over than some of the NHL squads from which these players have come.

"You have to trust your forwards when they have the puck, they'll make the right play and be strong on the puck. You don't want them making a blind pass or trying to put it through someone and put you in a bad situation. As a team you have to trust each other," Niedermayer said.

"We're definitely playing a lot better than we were at the beginning of the tournament. We have one more to go and we want to make that our best game yet. Playing in the gold medal game is something we'll never forget."

Team Canada's Eric Lindros (88) is sandwiched between Belarus players Oleg Khmyl, top, and Ruslan Salei during the second period of their semifinal men's hockey game.

Mario Lemieux (66) of Canada carries the puck into the Swedish zone in Game 1.

Lemieux, Yzerman Together Again at Last

Linemates getting more ice time than in 1983

PAUL HUNTER
The Toronto Star

WEST VALLEY CITY, Utah, Feb. 21, 2002 — How about this for a fourth line. Mario Lemieux in the middle with Steve Yzerman on his right and Dave Andreychuk on his left. That was the unit Canada had at its disposal at the 1983 world junior hockey championships.

"We didn't play much," Lemieux said with a chuckle yesterday. "We didn't see much ice at all."

Now, 19 years and 1,894 regular season goals later, two of the three have been reunited on Canada's top line here at the Olympics. It's the first time they've played together since and, yes, they're getting lots of ice time. And the results have been magical.

Lemieux and Yzerman combined for Canada's prettiest goal of the Games against Finland on Wednesday night when Yzerman passed to Lemieux in the slot and then drifted down the left

Steve Yzerman (19) of Canada races down the ice with the puck at the E Center in Salt Lake City.

wing for a surprise return pass that he buried into the open side.

"When you get the puck to Mario, good things happen," said Yzerman.

Lemieux says he remembers, even in his limited role at the '83 junior tournament, thinking that Yzerman was going to be an NHL star.

"He was a big star in junior but not a big guy," Lemieux said yesterday. "But I remember he had a lot of courage and he wanted to win really badly and that's what it takes to make it in the NHL."

The chemistry between the two has been fascinating to watch. It's almost as if each has an ingrained understanding of where the other will be on the ice at all times. Blind passes go tape to tape and each is there to help defensively on Canada's big line with Paul Kariya.

"We've watched each other play for the last 18 years so we kind of know each other's game and talent," said Lemieux. "So we just worry about trying to make good plays."

To anyone watching, however, it's obvious that Lemieux has that same desire to win that he spotted in Yzerman all those years ago. Despite a nagging hip injury, Lemieux has been quick to come back to his own end and he has even thrown a few bodychecks along the way.

"He has set the tone for us," said team general manager Wayne Gretzky, who set up Lemieux for one of the most memorable goals in Canadian hockey history to win the 1987 Canada Cup.

"Offensively, he's been a force while doing a lot of good things with the puck. And he's taken the man in our own zone," Gretzky explained.

"He's not punishing guys by any means, but he's getting in the way. Your leader has to show defensive abilities and show he's making commitment to it. We know Mario's power and strength is on offence, but he even blocked a shot (on Wednesday). He's doing little things in our end to motivate everyone else on our team to do it and that's what a leader does."

Team Canada Ends 50 Years of Frustration

'Now we're on top of the world,' goalie Brodeur exclaims

PAUL HUNTER
The Toronto Star

WEST VALLEY CITY, Utah, Feb. 24, 2002 — For a team, and for a hockey-obsessed nation, it was a giant group hug.

With strains of "O Canada" already wafting down from the rafters, an impromptu fan chorus washing away 50 years of Olympic frustration, goaltender Martin Brodeur was engulfed in a sea of red and white bodies that flooded off the bench.

The Canadians were gold-medal champs, the men matching what the women's team had achieved three nights earlier. A 5-2 win over the United States earned the country its record 17th medal of these Games.

Canada can breathe again.

Fifty years to the day after the Edmonton Mercury Hockey Club brought a gold medal home from Oslo, a group of diverse but impressive hockey talents, hailing from Burnaby, B.C., to Inverness, N.S., pulled together for the game of their lives.

And they gave a new generation of hockey fans their seminal moment. Their Summit Series. Their Canada Cup.

"Canadians talked about this tournament for a long time, this Olympic team and its selection," Brodeur said. "They took the roster apart. Put it together. Put us down. Said we were the best ever."

Brodeur followed in the footsteps of his father Denis, who was a bronze-medal winner as Canada's goaltender in 1956.

"Everyone knows about this team and now we're on top of the world," Brodeur added. "Now people will remember this lineup. Just like the '72 series or 1952 for older people."

In a dominant performance that was a complete reversal of how Canada played in a 5-2 loss to Sweden in its Olympic debut, Canada came hard at the Americans, mixing in-your-face forechecking with poise, skill and a determination that was both admirable and intimidating.

Game Summary

BOX SCORE

Canada	2	1	2	—	**5**
United States	1	1	0	—	**2**

FIRST PERIOD
1. USA, Amonte (Weight, Poti) 8:49
2. CAN, Kariya (Pronger, Lemieux) 14:54
3. CAN, Iginla (Sakic, Gagn/) 18:33
Penalties — CAN, Niedermayer (interference) 3:04, CAN, Fleury (cross-checking) 10:03.

SECOND PERIOD
4. USA, Rafalski (Modano) 15:30 (pp)
5. CAN, Sakic (Jovanovski, Blake) 18:19
Penalties — USA, Hull (hooking) 9:27, USA, Miller (high-sticking) 10:19, CAN, MacInnnis (interference) 14:40, USA, Roenick (tripping) 17:30.

THIRD PERIOD
6. CAN, Iginla (Yzerman, Sakic) 16:01
7. CAN, Sakic (Iginla) 18:40
Penalty — CAN, Yzerman (tripping) 13:43.

SHOTS ON GOAL

Canada	11	17	10	—	**38**
U.S.	10	14	9	—	**33**

Goal — Canada: Martin Brodeur (W, 4-0-1); United States: Mike Richter (L, 2-1-1).
Power-plays (goals-chances) - Canada: 1-3; U.S. 1-4.

"You could tell right from the start, just by looking at them, they meant business," said American centre Jeremy Roenick.

In just over a week, Team Canada went from smoked to smokin'. They followed that loss to Sweden with a mediocre 3-2 win over Germany and then a strong performance but just a 3-3 tie with the Czech Republic. Then it was an easy path to a tough

Goalie Martin Brodeur (30) celebrates with teammate Simon Gagne.

game with wins over Finland and Belarus before this gold-medal match with the United States.

The Canadians shrugged off the weight of a nation's hopes and expectations and erased the doubts that dogged them through their early play.

"We had to win and we knew we were going to win," said pint-sized winger Theo Fleury.

And win they did, backed by the high-flying line of Joe Sakic, who was named tournament most valuable player, Jarome Iginla and Simon Gagne. Iginla and Sakic each had two goals. Paul Kariya had the other.

"At the team meeting last night, we all talked about who would be the next Paul Henderson," said the team's executive director Wayne Gretzky, referring to the former Maple Leaf who scored the winner in 1972. "It was good, we had three guys with big goals today."

And when the fourth Canadian goal went in, a rocket from Iginla that American goalie Mike Richter couldn't handle with just under four minutes left, Gretzky began pumping his fist in his balcony perch overlooking centre ice. Then, with just over a minute remaining, Sakic scored his second. It was over.

"I don't know if you know what's it's like to have a piano on your back for the last 10 days but I tell you, somebody just lifted it off Team Canada," said defenceman Al MacInnis. "Nobody had the amount of pressure this team had coming into the tournament. The headlines coming into this tournament were: Gold or bust," added the oldest player on the squad at 38.

And when it was over, the players gathered in joyous celebration on the ice, breaking away from their congratulatory hugs to wave to the crowd to wave to family members in the crowd.

Joe Nieuwendyk found his 10-month daughter, Tyra, and brought her onto the ice. Mike Peca did the same with his young child. Owen Nolan grabbed a video camera to capture the moment. Even coach Pat Quinn did the oddest thing. He sought out referee Bill McCreary to shake his hand.

Lemieux did a brief twirl with a Canadian flag before the medal presentation but the chest-thumping was muted, probably out of respect for their opponents, who in many cases were either friends or NHL teammates.

"It was awesome, just an incredible feeling of accomplishment," said Nieuwendyk.

Martin Brodeur blocks John LeClair's shot as teammate Al MacInnis (2) slides into the net.

The Best on the Day it Mattered

DAMIEN COX
The Toronto Star

WEST VALLEY CITY, Utah, Feb. 24, 2002 — THE PLAN of attack was simple and ruthless.

Team Canada went into today's gold-medal game against the unbeaten U.S. with two main points of focus.

One, the coaching staff urged the players to sever the head of the American beast, to paralyze the talented forward units by hacking away the ability of the swift U.S. blue-line corps to move the puck up.

Second, Pat Quinn & Co. wanted the top American line of Mike Modano, John LeClair and Brett Hull to spend more time worrying about its defensive responsibilities than launching raids in the Canadian end.

Both objectives were accomplished, meaning that an enormous wave of Canadian emotion was channelled in the most productive way and created, on the day, a decisive superiority.

The U.S. was probably the best team in this Olympic tournament, but the Canadians were the best team on the day that mattered most.

For much of the day, the only issue that clouded that fact was the presence of goalie Mike Richter, who saved the U.S. from trailing by three or four by the second intermission.

Richter, however, couldn't stop aging U.S. defenders like Chris Chelios, Gary Suter and Phil Housley from being battered and hounded all afternoon by Canadian forwards.

"We felt we had to take advantage of their team down low," said Quinn. "They had tremendous skill at the back end and we didn't want to let them get involved."

Chelios was hit hard by Red Wings teammate Brendan Shanahan in the first period, a check that was followed up by a loud collision with Theo Fleury and then, surprisingly, a thump courtesy of captain Mario Lemieux.

Suter, meanwhile, had to compete physically deep in his own zone all day and couldn't handle power forward Jarome Iginla on a charge to the net in the first that resulted in Canada's second goal.

"Our pressure game was really good," said tourney MVP Joe Sakic.

Quinn and his coaching staff also forced Modano and friends in to play against the best Canadian lines.

Most of the night, the Modano unit had to compete head-to-head against either Lemieux between Steve Yzerman and Paul Kariya, or Sakic between swift youngsters Simon Gagne and Iginla.

Not surprisingly, the three U.S. forwards all ended up with minus-2 ratings. "It had a good effect," said Quinn.

When it was over, the Canadians had put five shots into the U.S. net, matching the collective offensive success of the Russians, Finns, Belarussians and Germans over the previous five tournament matches.

Quinn, who has never won a Stanley Cup as a coach, will clearly have a hard time letting go of this team when the 23 players scatter to their NHL squads today.

"It'll probably never happen again for me. It was a very special moment," he said. "I wish I could take this team and go barnstorming, become the Globetrotters."

He now returns to the task of getting the Maple Leafs deep into the Stanley Cup tournament, and part of the process will include bringing back Mats Sundin from Sweden's stunning loss at the hands of Belarus and mending fences with Curtis Joseph, who lost his shot at the starting job with Team Canada after just one game.

"(Joseph) is happy tonight but maybe he would have been happier if he had been in the net," said Quinn, who started Martin Brodeur against Germany in the second game of the tournament and never changed back.

"As we kept getting better, it was hard to change. But I love (Joseph). I think he's a terrific young guy."

That process of re-igniting the Leaf season resumes Tuesday night against Carolina.

Sigh. How all of us will return to NHL reality seems, at this moment, unfathomable.

Joe Sakic (91) stick handles past defenseman Aaron Miller (33) to the front for a wrap-around shot .

Canada's Jarome Iginla (12) celebrates after scoring the team's second goal on goalie Mike Richter (35) of the USA in the second period.

Jarome Iginla (12) of Canada celebrates his goal against the USA during the men's ice hockey gold medal game.

A Time for Veterans to Step to Fore

Sakic, Lemieux and Yzerman led way when going got tough

PAUL HUNTER
The Toronto Star

WEST VALLEY CITY, Utah, Feb. 24, 2002 — It was, according to Team Canada executive director Wayne Gretzky, in the losing that his squad learned how to win in the end.

It was during that disastrous 5-2 loss to Sweden that opened the tournament when the holy triumvirate of Canadian hockey stepped forward to show the leadership that would eventually carry the team to a gold medal today here.

"When it was 5-1 after the second period in that game, Mario Lemieux, Joe Sakic and Steve Yzerman moved to the forefront," said Gretzky.

"They didn't just throw their sticks out there in the third period, they played their hearts out and kept going. Mario was unbelievable for our team. Canada should be very proud of him."

In a tournament that was often about heart and persevering, it was the three veteran forwards who showed the way on and off the ice. Sakic, who was named tournament most valuable player, led Canada in both goals with four and points with seven.

Lemieux and Yzerman were second on the team in points, both finishing with two goals and four assists.

"This is the chance of a lifetime, to play in the Olympics and to have the chance to do something great for your country is awesome," said Lemieux.

"I was born in Canada. Once you are born there, you're always going to be Canadian and will always do what whatever you can for your country and that's what I did this week."

Canada did not have the services of Lemieux and Sakic, or Paul Kariya for that matter, at Nagano and their presence was a huge difference here.

Yzerman was there but he played a much more prominent role this time, skating on the top line with Lemieux and Kariya for Coach Pat Quinn.

"When things got a little tough early, the leadership on the team was so pervasive with Joe Sakic, Steve Yzerman and Mario Lemieux," said Quinn.

"Those were the guys buying in so the rest of us bought in."

On the ice, Lemieux was marvellous, although he left Canadian fans gasping when he missed a wide open net in the second period, a shot off the post that would have put Canada up, 3-1, instead the Americans came back to tie the game at 2-2.

"That's not something I've done too many times in my career," he said.

United States forward Jeremy Roenick said you could tell from Lemieux's reaction that his team was in trouble.

"I almost fainted when he missed that," said Roenick. "But he had that real look of determination after that."

American defenceman Chris Chelios thought it was Sakic who made the biggest difference in Canada's 5-2 victory.

"They won as a team but sometimes it takes one individual. Joe Sakic really stepped it up. There are guys on both teams that know what it takes to win but he had a heck of a game," said Chelios. "He's a great player and a great leader."

Lemieux actually made one of the most impressive plays of the night by not touching the puck.

On Kariya's goal, the first for Canada, Chris Pronger fired a pass to Lemieux in the slot.

But the big centre, aware that Kariya was to his left, let the puck drift between his legs to Kariya for an easy goal into the open side.

"(Lemieux) is sneaky. He has such a good hockey sense," said American goaltender Mike Richter. "He knows Kariya is there. I can see them both and the pass goes to Mario's stick. He doesn't just not play it, he actually puts his stick there to play it and then moves his stick. It was a beautiful play — a play you have to honour as a goalie."

Yzerman was thrilled at the outcome.

"It's (winning the gold medal) is going to be remembered for a long time," explained Yzerman. "I've got to imagine the whole country was watching. It's a proud moment for everyone."

Above: U.S. goalkeeper Mike Richter (35) can not make the save on a shot for a goal by Team Canada's Joe Sakic. Sakic's goal gave Team Canada a 5-2 lead late in the third period. Below: Steve Yzerman (9) of Canada is checked into the glass in the men's ice hockey gold medal game against the U.S.

Above: Brendan Shanahan (14) celebrates with teammate Jarome Iginla. Below left: Team captain Mario Lemeiux enjoys a victory lap. Below right: Janet and Wayne Gretzky savor the celebration.

The members of Team Canada were awarded their gold medals following the 5-2 win against the U.S. Afterward, Theo Fleury (below right) led the long-awaited victory party.

He could be forgiven for dreading a return to the seeming drudgery of the NHL regular season, but Quinn said he's now got his eyes on another championship — bringing the Stanley Cup to Toronto.

"The Cup has been my dream. That's why I've spent so long in this game," said Quinn, who's confident he'll get a full effort from the seven Leaf players returning from the Olympics. Among them are a pair of players who both had less than satisfying Olympic experiences — Leaf captain Mats Sundin and star netminder Curtis Joseph.

Sundin was one of the best forwards at the Olympics, but was devastated when his Swedish national team was upset in the quarterfinals by unheralded Belarus. Quinn doesn't think Sundin will take long to bounce back.

"The only thing I know about Mats is that he's gotten better and more mature during his entire time here. I don't doubt for a minute he'll be ready," said Quinn, who also had to disappoint Joseph by yanking him after a disastrous tournament-opening 5-2 loss to Sweden.

It was tough to make the call said Quinn, who insisted the loss wasn't Joseph's fault.

"I think he played well. He's a proud guy and I'm sure he wanted to play the whole time," said Quinn.

Team Canada coach Pat Quinn relishes his team's 5-2 defeat of the U.S. in the men's ice hockey gold medal game of the Winter Olympic Games at the E Center in Salt Lake City, Utah.

Team Canada 2002 Roster

PLAYER	S/C	HT	WT	BIRTHDATE	HOMETOWN	2000-01 CLUB
Goaltenders						
20 Ed Belfour	L/G	5' 11	192	04/21/65	Carman, MB	Dallas Stars
30 Martin Brodeur	L/G	6' 2	205	05/06/72	Montreal, QC	New Jersey Devils
31 Curtis Joseph	L/G	5' 11	190	04/29/67	Keswick, ON	Toronto Maple Leafs
Defence						
4 Rob Blake*	R/D	6' 4	227	12/10/69	Simcoe, ON	Colorado Avalanche
3 Eric Brewer	L/G	6' 3	220	04/17/79	Kamloops, BC	Edmonton Oilers
52 Adam Foote	R/D	6' 2	215	07/10/71	Whitby, ON	Colorado Avalanche
55 Ed Jovanovski	L/G	6' 2	210	06/26/76	Windsor, ON	Vancouver Canucks
2 Al MacInnis	R/D	6' 2	209	07/11/63	Port Hood , NS	St. Louis Blues
27 Scott Niedermayer*	L/G	6' 1	200	08/31/73	Cranbrook, BC	New Jersey Devils
44 Chris Pronger*	L/G	6' 6	220	10/10/74	Dryden, ON	St. Louis Blues
Forwards						
74 Theoren Fleury	R/D	5' 6	180	06/29/68	Russel, MB	New York Rangers
21 Simon Gagné	L/G	6' 0	190	02/29/80	Ste-Foy, QC	Philadelphia Flyers
12 Jarome Iginla	L/G	6' 1	202	07/01/77	Edmonton, AB	Calgary Flames
9 Paul Kariya*	L/G	5' 10	173	10/16/74	Vancouver, BC	Anaheim Mighty Ducks
66 Mario Lemieux*	R/D	6' 4	225	10/05/65	Montreal, QC	Pittsburgh Penguins
88 Eric Lindros	R/D	6' 4	236	02/28/73	Toronto, ON	New York Rangers
25 Joe Nieuwendyk	L/G	6' 1	205	09/10/66	Whitby, ON	Dallas Stars
11 Owen Nolan*	R/D	6' 1	210	02/12/72	Thorold, ON	San Jose Sharks
37 Michael Peca	R/D	5' 11	190	03/26/74	Toronto, ON	New York Islanders
91 Joe Sakic*	L/G	5' 11	195	07/07/69	Burnaby, BC	Colorado Avalanche
14 Brendan Shanahan	L/G	6' 3	220	01/23/69	Mimico, ON	Detroit Red Wings
94 Ryan Smyth	L/G	6' 1	195	02/21/76	Banff, AB	Edmonton Oilers
19 Steve Yzerman*	R/D	5' 11	185	05/09/65	Nepean, ON	Detroit Red Wings

* Denotes players who were officially named to Canada's 2002 Olympic Team on March 23, 2001

Team Canada Personnel

President, CHA/ACH: Bob Nicholson; CHA/ACH
Executive Director: Wayne Gretzky, Phoenix Coyotes
Assistant Executive Director: Kevin Lowe,
    Edmonton Oilers
Dir., Player Personnel: Steve Tambellini,
    Vancouver Canucks
Head Coach: Pat Quinn, Toronto Maple Leafs
Associate Coach: Ken Hitchcock, Dallas Stars
Associate Coach: Jacques Martin, Ottawa Senators
Associate Coach: Wayne Fleming, CHA/ACH
Video Coach: Mike Pelino, CHA/ACH
Equipment Manager: Barrie Stafford,
    Edmonton Oilers

Equipment Manager: Pierre Gervais,
    Montreal Canadiens
Team Doctor: Dr. Jim Thorne, CHA/ACH
Athletic Therapist: Ken Lowe, Edmonton Oilers
Athletic Therapist: Jim Ramsay, New York Rangers
Masseuse: Stewart Poirier, Edmonton Oilers
Masseuse: Tom Plasko, Pittsburgh Penguins
Dir., Media Relations: Brad Pascall, CHA/ACH
Manager, Media Relations: Bill Tuele,
    Edmonton Oilers
Manager, Media Relations: Andre Brin, CHA/ACH
Team Leader: Johnny Misley, CHA/ACH
Team Leader: Denis Hainault, CHA/ACH